1969 U.K.

YEARBOOK

ISBN: 9781790423996

This book gives a fascinating and informative insight into life in the United Kingdom in 1969. It includes everything from the most popular music of the year to the cost of a buying a new house. Additionally there are chapters covering people in high office, the best-selling films of the year and all the main news and events. Want to know which team won the FA Cup or which British personalities were born in 1969? All this and much more awaits you within.

INDEX

	Page
Calendar	4
People In High Office	5
British News & Events	9
Worldwide News & Events	18
Births - UK Personalities	21
Notable British Deaths	26
Popular Music	28
Top 5 Films	34
Sporting Winners	50
Cost Of Living	57
Cartoons	65

FIRST EDITION

1969

January

M	T	W	T	F	S	S
		1	2	3	4	5
6	7	8	9	10	11	12
13	14	15	16	17	18	19
20	21	22	23	24	25	26
27	28	29	30	31		

○:3 ◑:11 ●:18 ◐:25

February

M	T	W	T	F	S	S
					1	2
3	4	5	6	7	8	9
10	11	12	13	14	15	16
17	18	19	20	21	22	23
24	25	26	27	28		

○:2 ◑:10 ●:16 ◐:24

March

M	T	W	T	F	S	S
					1	2
3	4	5	6	7	8	9
10	11	12	13	14	15	16
17	18	19	20	21	22	23
24	25	26	27	28	29	30
31						

○:4 ◑:11 ●:18 ◐:26

April

M	T	W	T	F	S	S
	1	2	3	4	5	6
7	8	9	10	11	12	13
14	15	16	17	18	19	20
21	22	23	24	25	26	27
28	29	30				

○:2 ◑:9 ●:16 ◐:24

May

M	T	W	T	F	S	S
			1	2	3	4
5	6	7	8	9	10	11
12	13	14	15	16	17	18
19	20	21	22	23	24	25
26	27	28	29	30	31	

○:2 ◑:8 ●:16 ◐:24 ○:31

June

M	T	W	T	F	S	S
						1
2	3	4	5	6	7	8
9	10	11	12	13	14	15
16	17	18	19	20	21	22
23	24	25	26	27	28	29
30						

◑:7 ●:15 ◐:23 ○:29

July

M	T	W	T	F	S	S
	1	2	3	4	5	6
7	8	9	10	11	12	13
14	15	16	17	18	19	20
21	22	23	24	25	26	27
28	29	30	31			

◑:6 ●:14 ◐:22 ○:29

August

M	T	W	T	F	S	S
				1	2	3
4	5	6	7	8	9	10
11	12	13	14	15	16	17
18	19	20	21	22	23	24
25	26	27	28	29	30	31

◑:5 ●:13 ◐:20 ○:27

September

M	T	W	T	F	S	S
1	2	3	4	5	6	7
8	9	10	11	12	13	14
15	16	17	18	19	20	21
22	23	24	25	26	27	28
29	30					

◑:3 ●:11 ◐:19 ○:25

October

M	T	W	T	F	S	S
	1	2	3	4	5	
6	7	8	9	10	11	12
13	14	15	16	17	18	19
20	21	22	23	24	25	26
27	28	29	30	31		

◑:3 ●:11 ◐:18 ○:25

November

M	T	W	T	F	S	S
					1	2
3	4	5	6	7	8	9
10	11	12	13	14	15	16
17	18	19	20	21	22	23
24	25	26	27	28	29	30

◑:2 ●:9 ◐:16 ○:24

December

M	T	W	T	F	S	S
1	2	3	4	5	6	7
8	9	10	11	12	13	14
15	16	17	18	19	20	21
22	23	24	25	26	27	28
29	30	31				

◑:2 ●:9 ◐:16 ○:23 ◑:31

PEOPLE IN HIGH OFFICE

Monarch - Queen Elizabeth II
Reign: 6th February 1952 - Present
Predecessor: King George VI
Heir Apparent: Charles, Prince Of Wales

United Kingdom

Prime Minister - Harold Wilson
Labour Party
16th October 1964 - 19th June 1970

New Zealand

Ireland

United States

Prime Minister
Keith Holyoake
12th December 1960 -
7th February 1972

Taoiseach
Jack Lynch
10th November 1966 -
14th March 1973

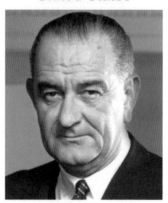

President
Richard Nixon
20th January 1969 -
9th August 1974

Australia

Prime Minister
John Gorton (1968-1971)

Brazil

President
Artur da Costa e Silva (1967-1969)
Military Junta (1969)
Emílio Garrastazú Médici (1969-1974)

Canada

Prime Minister
Pierre Trudeau (1968-1979)

China

Communist Party Leader
Mao Zedong (1935-1976)

France

President
Charles de Gaulle (1959-1969)
Alain Poher (1969)
Georges Pompidou (1969-1974)

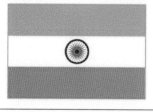

India

Prime Minister
Indira Gandhi (1966-1977)

Israel

Prime Minister
Levi Eshkol (1963-1969)
Yigal Allon (1969)
Golda Meir (1969-1974)

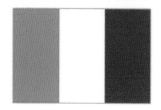

Italy

Prime Minister
Mariano Rumor (1968-1970)

	Japan	Prime Minister Eisaku Satō (1964-1972)
	Mexico	President Gustavo Díaz Ordaz (1964-1970)
	Pakistan	President Ayub Khan (1958-1969) Yahya Khan (1969-1971)

South Africa — Prime Minister B. J. Vorster (1966-1978)

Soviet Union — Communist Party Leader Leonid Brezhnev (1964-1982)

Spain — Prime Minister Francisco Franco (1938-1973)

Turkey — Prime Minister Süleyman Demirel (1965-1971)

West Germany — Chancellor Kurt Georg Kiesinger (1966-1969) Willy Brandt (1969-1974)

BRITISH NEWS & EVENTS

JAN

2nd | The Space Hopper is introduced to the UK at the Brighton Toy Fair.

Australian media mogul Rupert Murdoch beats off a £34 million offer from Robert Maxwell's Pergamon Press to win control of the News Of The World newspaper group.

4th | Guitarist and singer Jimi Hendrix is banned from the BBC after playing an impromptu version of Cream's 'Sunshine Of Your Love' on the BBC One programme Happening for Lulu.

4th | On the fourth and final day of the People's Democracy (PD) march from Claudy to Derry, the Royal Ulster Constabulary (RUC) breaks up a rally that is being held in the centre of Derry as the march arrives. This action, and the subsequent entry of the RUC into the Bogside area of the city, leads to serious rioting and over one hundred injuries.

5th | Ariana Afghan Airlines Flight 701 crashes into a house in heavy fog on its approach to London's Gatwick Airport. Forty-eight of the Boeing 727's sixty-two passengers are killed, as well as two adult occupants of the house; a baby present in the house suffers only minor injuries.

6th January - The final passenger train traverses the Waverley Line which runs south from Edinburgh, through Midlothian and the Scottish Borders, to Carlisle. The line, nicknamed after the immensely popular Waverley Novels written by Sir Walter Scott, was closed a result of the Beeching Report. *Photo: A Waverley Line Tour train at St Boswells Station in 1961.*

11th | Further rioting occurs in a number of areas of Northern Ireland, particularly in Derry and Newry.

14th | Sir Matt Busby announces his retirement at the end of the season as manager of Manchester United F.C. After 24 years in charge he is to become a director at the club and hand over first-team duties to current first team trainer, and former player, Wilf McGuinness.

15th	Terence O'Neill, the Northern Ireland Prime Minister, announces the setting up of an official inquiry into the disturbances in Derry and elsewhere. The inquiry, under the chairmanship of Scottish judge Lord Cameron, is to look into the causes of the civil unrest.
18th	Pete Best wins his defamation lawsuit against the Beatles and Playboy magazine. He had originally sought $8,000,000 but settles out of court for an undisclosed sum.
24th	A violent protest by students, caused by the installation of steel security gates, closes the London School of Economics for three weeks.
24th	Ford launches the Capri at the Brussels Motor Show, a four-seater sports coupe designed to compete with the likes of British Leyland's MGB. *Fun Fact: The Capri went on to be a highly successful car for Ford, selling nearly 1.9 million units by the time production stopped at the end of 1986.*

30th January - The Beatles - John Lennon, Paul McCartney, George Harrison and Ringo Starr - play live for one last time with an impromptu gig on the roof of their Apple headquarters in Saville Row, Mayfair, London. The outing is abruptly cut short by police who object to the noise, but not before they manage to thrill Londoners on adjacent rooftops and on the streets below. The 42-minute rooftop 'concert' was the first live gig since the band stopped touring in 1966 and ends with Lennon quipping, "I hope we passed the audition".

FEB

18th	Pop star Lulu, 20, gets married to 19-year old Maurice Gibb of the Bee Gees at St. James Church, Gerrards Cross, Buckinghamshire. The celebrity couple split up just four years later after Maurice's rock and roll lifestyle had started to take its toll on their marriage.

MAR

	The first B&Q DIY superstore is opened by Richard Block and David Quayle in a disused cinema on Portswood Road, Southampton. Although initially called Block and Quayle the stores name was soon shortened to B&Q.
2nd	The Anglo-French supersonic airliner Concorde makes its maiden flight after two previous attempts were aborted due to bad weather. Spontaneous applause and cheers broke out from observers as the French-built prototype of the supersonic transport (SST) took off from Toulouse Airport at around 3.30pm; it circled for just 27 minutes before landing due to further weather concerns. Test pilot Andre Turcat said that the flight was "as perfect as we had expected", but warned that Concorde was far from being the finished article.

4th	The Kray twins, Ronnie and Reggie, are both found guilty of murdering Jack 'the Hat' McVitie; Ronnie was also found guilty of murdering George Cornell. A day later they are sentenced to life imprisonment by Mr Justice Melford Stevenson with a recommended minimum of thirty years - the sentences are the longest ever passed at the Old Bailey for murder. The Kray's elder brother, Charles, was also found guilty and jailed for 10 years for being an accessory in the murder of McVitie.
7th	The official opening ceremony of London Underground's Victoria Line takes place at Victoria station. The Queen unveils a commemorative plaque on the station concourse and, after the short ceremony, proceeds to buy a 5d ticket and travel to Green Park. In so doing she becomes the first reigning monarch to ride on the London Underground.
12th	Paul McCartney marries Linda Eastman at Marylebone Register Office in London. The registry office had been booked the previous day and McCartney had bought a £12 ring 'just before the shop shut'.
17th	The Longhope lifeboat T.G.B. from Orkney capsizes after answering a mayday call during severe storms. All eight crew members are lost.
19th	A 135 strong contingent of 2nd Battalion the Parachute Regiment, and 40 Metropolitan Police officers, 'invade' the island of Anguilla to restore order after British envoy William Whitlock had been expelled some 8 days earlier. The invasion, code-named Operation Sheepskin, was a badly kept secret and was greeted by a horde of foreign journalists and a completely demilitarised local populace.

19th March - The 386 metre (1,266ft) tall Emley Moor transmitting station television mast in West Yorkshire collapses. The cause is attributed to a combination of strong winds and the weight of ice that had formed around the top of the mast and guy wires. Although a falling stay cable cut through a local church and across the transmitter site buildings, no one was injured. *Fun Fact: At the time of its construction in 1966, the Emley Moor mast was one of the tallest man-made structures in the world.*

25th	John Lennon and Yoko Ono get married at the British Consulate Office in Gibraltar.

MAR

25th	The Northern Irish hard line Protestant leader Reverend Ian Paisley and Major Ronald Bunting are jailed for organising an illegal counter-demonstration (against a civil rights march in Armagh); they are released on the 6th May during a general amnesty for people convicted of political offences.
27th	Catherine McConnachie becomes the first woman to be ordained in the Church of Scotland (by the Presbytery of Aberdeen).
29th	Lulu, representing the UK with the song 'Boom Bang-a-Bang', shares first place in the Eurovision Song Contest in a four-way tie with France, the Netherlands and the host country, Spain.

APR

	The Raleigh Chopper children's 'wheelie' bike was launched in the UK.
1st	The Hawker Siddeley Harrier GR.1 V/STOL 'Jump Jet' fighter enters in to service with the RAF.
9th	Sikh busmen in Wolverhampton win the right to wear turbans on duty after a long-running campaign. Wolverhampton's Transport Committee dropped its ban after the leader of a Sikh group, Sohan Singh Jolly, had threatened to burn himself to death in protest.
17th	The Representation of the People Act lowers the voting age from 21 to 18 with effect from February 1970. It also permits candidates to have a party label included on the ballot paper, and removes the right (theoretically restored in 1967) of convicted prisoners to vote in Parliamentary elections.
17th	Bernadette Devlin wins the Mid Ulster by-election and becomes the youngest ever female MP at 21 years old. *Fun Fact: Devlin remained the youngest female MP until the May 2015 general election when 20-year-old Scottish SNP politician Mhairi Black broke her record.*

22nd April - Robin Knox-Johnston becomes the first person to perform a single-handed non-stop circumnavigation of the globe. Of the 9 competitors in Sunday Times Golden Globe Race he was the only finisher, and was awarded both the trophy and £5,000 prize money.

24th	The British Leyland Motor Corporation launches Britain's first production hatchback car, the Austin Maxi, in Oporto, Portugal. Launched in a blaze of publicity it was designed to compete with family saloons like the Ford Cortina.

APR

24th	The final episode of the long-running serial drama Mrs Dale's Diary is broadcast; it was first aired on the 5th January 1948, on the BBC Light Programme.
26th	Manchester City wins the FA Cup final with a 1-0 defeat over Leicester City in front of 100,000 fans at Wembley Stadium.
28th	Leeds United win the Football League First Division title for the first time in their history. They wrap up the title race with a 0-0 draw against Liverpool, and finish the season with an unbeaten home record.

MAY

2nd May - Cunard's ocean liner Queen Elizabeth 2 departs Southampton on her maiden voyage to New York. The ship was built by John Brown and Company at their shipyard in Clydebank, Scotland, for an agreed price of £25,427,000. She was launched and named on the 20th September 1967 by Queen Elizabeth II using the same pair of gold scissors her mother and grandmother had used to launch Queen Elizabeth and Queen Mary respectively. On the 3rd May 1982 she was requisitioned by the British government for service as a troop carrier in the Falklands War and since the 18th April 2018 has been operating as a floating hotel in Dubai. *Photo: The QE2, on her maiden voyage, arriving in New York from Southampton on the 7th May 1969.*

23rd	The Who release their fourth studio album, the concept album Tommy. *Fun Fact: Tommy has to date sold over 20 million copies globally.*
29th	The film Carry On Camping is released and features many series regulars such as Sid James, Kenneth Williams, Charles Hawtrey, Joan Sims, Terry Scott, Hattie Jacques, Barbara Windsor, Bernard Bresslaw and Peter Butterworth. With a budget of £208,354 it is the seventeenth in the series of Carry On films to be made.

JUN

14th	The black RCMP Police Service Horse, Burmese, ridden by the Queen, makes her first appearance at Trooping the Colour; she would continue in this role until 1986.

JUN

21st	A documentary entitled Royal Family is broadcast and gives audiences an unprecedented view of a year in the private and public life of the Queen and her family. The 110 minute film is shown with a two minute tea break interval, and is watched by 23 million people. *Fun Fact: A co-production with ITV, Royal Family was sold around the world and was seen by an estimated audience of 350 million.*
21st	Dr Who: Patrick Troughton makes his final appearance as the Second Doctor after three series and 119 episodes; the episode is the last Dr Who made in black and white and is watched by 5 million viewers.
22nd	American singer, actress, dancer and vaudevillian Judy Garland, aged 47, dies of a drug overdose in her London home.
30th	Alwyn Jones and George Taylor, two members of the Mudiad Amddiffyn Cymru (Movement for the Defence of Wales), are killed whilst placing a bomb outside government offices in Abergele (in an attempt to disrupt the investiture of Prince Charles the following day).

JUL

1st July - Prince Charles is invested with his title, Prince of Wales, at a ceremony in Caernarfon (he was actually created Prince of Wales and Earl of Chester by Letters Patent on the 26th July 1958). The investiture was watched by millions on television, and attracted large and excited crowds in Caernarfon, but it also aroused considerable hostility among a minority of nationalist and republican Welsh people. Prince Charles had spent ten weeks leading up to his investiture learning about Welsh culture and language, and during the ceremony he gave his replies in both English and Welsh.

1st	Whilst on holiday John Lennon, Yoko Ono and their children are hospitalised at Golspie in Scotland after Lennon crashed his white British Leyland Austin Maxi in the Highlands near Durness.

JUL

3rd — Swansea is granted city status to mark Prince Charles's investiture as the Prince of Wales. The Prince made the announcement during a tour of Wales.

10th — Donald Crowhurst's trimaran, Teignmouth Electron, is found drifting and unoccupied mid-Atlantic. Crowhurst had been competing in the Sunday Times Golden Globe Race won by Robin Knox-Johnston. It is discovered that Crowhurst had been falsifying his positions and had ultimately committed suicide at sea. The journey was meticulously catalogued in Crowhurst's logbooks, which also documented the captain's thoughts, philosophy, and eventual mental breakdown.

19th — British rower and adventurer John Fairfax lands in Hollywood Beach, Florida, and becomes the first person to row across an ocean solo; he had left Gran Canaria on the 20th January and had spent a total of 180 days at sea on board the 25ft ocean rowboat Britannia.

23rd — BBC Two television airs the first Pot Black snooker tournament. The programme helps transform snooker from a minority sport, with just a handful of professionals, into one of the most popular sports in the United Kingdom.

24th — British lecturer Gerald Brooke is freed from a Soviet prison in exchange for the Soviet spies Morris and Lona Cohen. Brooke had been arrested in 1965 by KGB agents and sentenced to five years detention (including four years in labour camps) for smuggling anti-Soviet leaflets.

AUG

1st — The (pre-decimal) halfpenny, first minted in 1672, ceases to be legal tender.

8th — At 11:35am photographer Iain Macmillan takes a photo of The Beatles for their new album on a zebra crossing outside EMI Studios in Abbey Road. *Fun Fact: In December 2010 the crossing was given grade II listed status for its 'cultural and historical importance'.*

12th — Rioting breaks out in Derry, Northern Ireland in the Battle of the Bogside, the first major confrontation of The Troubles.

13th — The Taoiseach of the Republic of Ireland, Jack Lynch, makes a speech on RTÉ television stating that his government "can no longer stand by and see innocent people injured and perhaps worse". He also says that the Stormont government is no longer in control of the situation and that London should request the United Nations send a peacekeeping force to Northern Ireland.

14th — The British Government sends troops into Northern Ireland in what it says is a 'limited operation' to restore law and order. It follows three days and two nights of violence in the mainly-Catholic Bogside area of Londonderry.

30th — The Isle of Wight Festival begins and attracts an audience of 150,000 pop music fans over the 3 days of the event. It is the second of three music festivals to be held on the island between 1968 and 1970, and includes acts such as Bob Dylan, The Band, The Who, Free, Joe Cocker, The Bonzo Dog Band and The Moody Blues.

SEP

11th — The housing charity Shelter releases a report claiming that there are up to 3,000,000 people in need of rehousing because they are living in damp, overcrowded slum conditions.

21st — In a high-profile Metropolitan Police operation, squatters of the London Street Commune (a movement highlighting concerns about rising levels of homelessness) are evicted from 144 Piccadilly.

28th — The National Trust acquires ownership of the island of Lundy thanks to a donation covering the full purchase price from British millionaire Jack Hayward.

OCT

1st	The General Post Office (GPO), officially established in England in 1660 by Charles II, is abolished and the assets transferred to the newly-created Post Office Corporation.
4th	They're Off, an ITV television programme showing live coverage of horse racing is aired for the first time. In the early 1970s it is renamed The ITV Seven, reflecting the number of races shown each week.
5th	Monty Python's Flying Circus first episode is broadcast on the BBC. It stars Terry Jones, Michael Palin, Eric Idle, John Cleese, Graham Chapman and American-born Terry Gilliam.
13th	Miners go on an unofficial strike with 140 of the 307 collieries owned by the National Coal Board involved (it includes all collieries in the Yorkshire area). The strike lasts for roughly two weeks, with some pits returning to work before others.
14th	The new seven-sided 50p coin is introduced as replacement for the 10-shilling note. It is the third decimal coin to be introduced into the British currency which is due to go totally decimal on the 15th February 1971, to be known as D-Day. It receives a mixed reception from the British public with many people complaining that it was easily confused with the 10p coin. *Fun Fact: The Decimal Currency Board (DCB) had stockpiled 120 million 50-pence coins at banks around the country ready for the introduction of the coin, making it the largest ever issue of a new coin. Chairman of the DCB Lord Fiske explained "the reason for this was to replace the 200 million ten-bob notes as soon as possible".*
16th	Peter Nichols' play The National Health premiers at the Old Vic in London. The black comedy proves to be a critical and commercial success, and is named Best New Play by the Evening Standard.

NOV

Ken Loach's film Kes, which is based on the 1968 novel A Kestrel for a Knave written by the Barnsley-born author Barry Hines, is released at the London Film Festival. *Fun Fact: In 1999 Kes was ranked seventh in the British Film Institute's Top Ten (British) Films of the 20th century.*

16th November - BBC1 makes its first broadcast of the children's television series Clangers. Made by Oliver Postgate and Peter Firmin's 'Smallfilms' using stop motion animation, it features creatures who live on, and inside, a small moon-like planet. They speak only in whistles and eat only green soup (supplied by the Soup Dragon) and blue string pudding. The programme, originally broadcast on BBC from 1969 to 1972, was re-commissioned by them in 2015.

17th	The Sun newspaper is relaunched as a tabloid under the ownership of Rupert Murdoch; the new shape papers' first front page headline is 'Horse Dope Sensation'.

NOV

19th The Benny Hill Show, first broadcast on the BBC in 1955, premieres on Thames Television. The show would run until 1989 before it is cancelled due to declining (UK) ratings and the large production costs of £450,000 per episode. *Fun Facts: At its peak in 1977 over 21 million viewers watched the Benny Hill Show. By 1989, when it was cancelled, it was being aired in 97 countries around the world.*

21st The controversial London Weekend Television comedy Curry and Chips, starring Spike Milligan and Eric Sykes, begins airing. It is pulled off air after six episodes following a ruling by the Independent Television Authority that it is racist, although confusingly the original ambition of the show was to highlight discrimination rather than promote it.

I am returning this MBE in protest against Britain's involvement in the Nigeria-Biafra thing, against our support of America in Vietnam and against Cold Turkey slipping down the charts.

with love John Lennon.

John Lennon   of Bag

25th November - John Lennon returns his MBE in protest against the British government's involvement in Biafra, their support of the U.S. war in Vietnam, and the disappointing performance of his second solo single Cold Turkey. *Photo: A draft (valued at £60,000) of the letter sent by Lennon when he returned his MBE; the actual letter remains in the Royal archives.*

DEC

10th Derek Barton jointly wins the Nobel Prize in Chemistry with Norwegian Odd Hassel 'for their contributions to the development of the concept of conformation and its application in chemistry'.

15th Barclays purchases Martins Bank and all its 700 branches.

18th The sixth James Bond film, On Her Majesty's Secret Service, premieres at the Odeon Leicester Square in London. It stars Australian actor George Lazenby as Bond alongside 31-year old Yorkshire-born Avengers actress Diana Rigg.

26th A fire breaks out at the 16th century Rose and Crown Hotel in Saffron Walden, Essex. The blaze starts in the early hours and at its height is attended by 75 firemen. The Christmas night tragedy results in the deaths of eleven people.

BRITISH PUBLICATIONS FIRST PRINTED IN 1969

- Kingsley Amis's novel The Green Man.
- Agatha Christie's Hercule Poirot novel Hallowe'en Party.
- John Fowles' novel The French Lieutenant's Woman.
- George MacDonald Fraser's novel Flashman.
- P. H. Newby's novel Something to Answer For.
- Children of Albion: Poetry of the Underground in Britain, edited by Michael Horovitz.

1. 15th January - The Soviet Union launches Soyuz 5, which docks with Soyuz 4 the following day for a transfer of crew. It is the first-ever docking of two manned spacecraft and the first-ever transfer of crew from one space vehicle to another; it is also the only time a transfer has been accomplished with a spacewalk. The two spacecraft undock and return to Earth on the 18th January.

2. 20th January - Richard Nixon is sworn in as the 37th President of the United States.

3. 22nd January - An assassination attempt is carried out on Leonid Brezhnev by deserter Viktor Ilyin. One person is killed and several are injured; Brezhnev escapes unharmed.

4. 4th February - Yasser Arafat is elected Palestine Liberation Organization leader at the Palestinian National Congress held in Cairo.

5. 9th February - The Boeing 747 'jumbo jet' makes its maiden flight after taking off from the Boeing airfield in Everett, Washington. Test pilots Jack Waddell and Brien Wygle were at the controls with Jess Wallick at the flight engineer's station.

6. 3rd March - NASA launches Apollo 9 carrying crew members James McDivitt (Commander), David Scott (Command Module Pilot), and Rusty Schweickart (Lunar Module Pilot). They spend ten days in low Earth orbit testing several aspects critical to accomplishing a successful moon landing - testing includes the Lunar Module engines, backpack life support systems, navigation systems, and docking manoeuvres.

7. 16th March - Viasa Flight 742 hits a series of power lines shortly after taking off for Miami and crashes into a neighbourhood in Maracaibo, Venezuela; all 84 people on board the DC-9 jet are killed, along with 71 people on the ground.

8. 17th March - Golda Meir becomes the first female prime minister of Israel.

9. April 4 - American heart surgeon Dr. Denton Cooley implants the first temporary artificial heart in to the chest of Haskell Karp, 47, of Skokie, Illinois, United States. Karp survives for 65 hours after the operation.

10. 28th April - Charles de Gaulle steps down as president of France after suffering defeat in a referendum the day before. The proposed referendum reforms, rejected by 52.4% of voters, would have led to government decentralisation and changes to the Senate.

11. 16th May - Venera 5, a Soviet atmospheric spaceprobe weighing 405kg (893lb), is jettisoned from its main spacecraft on its way towards the surface of Venus. A parachute opens to slow the rate of descent and for 53 minutes data from the Venusian atmosphere is returned. The probe finally succumbs to high temperatures and pressure as it nears the surface of Venus.

12. 18th May - NASA's Apollo 10 space mission is launched with a 3-man crew consisting of Thomas P. Stafford (Commander), John W. Young (Command Module Pilot), and Eugene A. Cernan (Lunar Module Pilot). The flight is a test run for the first Moon landing and successfully tests all aspects of a lunar landing, except the actual landing. The crew conducted a lunar orbit and lunar descent to about 9 miles from the surface before returning to Earth after 8 days. *Fun Fact: Apollo 10 set the record for the highest speed ever attained by a manned vehicle on its return from the Moon: 24,791mph on 26th May 1969.*

13. 3rd June - While operating at sea on SEATO manoeuvres, the Australian aircraft carrier HMAS Melbourne accidentally rams and slices into the American destroyer USS Frank E. Evans in the South China Sea killing 74 American seamen.

14. 20th June - Georges Pompidou is elected President of France. He would remain as President of the French Republic until his death on the 2nd April 1974.

15. 30th June - The Government of Spain formally returns the territory Ifni to Morocco.

16. 14th July - The Football War (also known as the 100 Hour War) begins when the Salvadoran military launches an attack against Honduras after existing tensions between the two countries coincided with rioting during a 1970 FIFA World Cup qualifier.

17. 16th July - Apollo 11 astronauts Neil Armstrong (Commander), Michael Collins (Command Module Pilot) and Buzz Aldrin (Lunar Module Pilot) are launched by a 363ft tall Saturn V rocket toward the Moon from Kennedy Space Center on Merritt Island, Florida. After travelling for three days they enter into lunar orbit and on the 20th July Armstrong and Aldrin transfer into the lunar module Eagle. Eagle then descends to the Moon's surface and lands in the Sea of Tranquility. On the 21st July, six hours after landing, an estimated 500 million people worldwide watch in awe as Neil Armstrong steps off Eagle's footpad onto the Moon and utters the now famous words, "That's one small step for [a] man, one giant leap for mankind". Twenty minutes after taking his historic first steps on the Moon he is joined by Buzz Aldrin and they proceed to collect 21.5kg (47.5lb) of lunar material to bring back to Earth. Armstrong and Aldrin spend a total of 21.5 hours on the Moon's surface before re-joining Michael Collins in the orbiting command module Columbia. The astronauts then jettison Eagle before blasting out on a trajectory back to Earth. They splash down in the Pacific Ocean on the 24th July and are immediately placed in biological isolation for several days (on the off chance they may have brought back germs from the Moon).

In recognition of their achievement the Apollo 11 crew rode in parades through New York, Chicago, and Los Angeles on the 13th August. Whilst in Los Angeles there was also an official State Dinner at the Century Plaza Hotel to celebrate the flight. It was attended by members of Congress, 44 governors, the Chief Justice of the United States and ambassadors from 83 nations. President Richard Nixon and Vice President Spiro T. Agnew honoured each astronaut by presenting them with the Presidential Medal of Freedom. This day of celebration was the beginning of a 45-day 'Giant Leap' tour which would take the astronauts to 25 foreign countries and include visits with many prominent world leaders.

18. 31st July - Elvis Presley performs his first live concert in 8 years in front of 2,000 people at the International Hotel, Las Vegas.

19. 5th August - NASA's Mariner 7, whose mission goal was to study the surface and atmosphere of Mars, makes its closest fly-by of the planet - 2,130mi (3,430km).

20. 9th August - Members of Manson Family invade the home of actress Sharon Tate and her husband Roman Polanski in Los Angeles. The followers kill Tate and her friends; Folgers coffee heiress Abigail Folger, Wojciech Frykowski, Hollywood hairstylist Jay Sebring and Steven Parent, who was visiting the Polanski's caretaker.

21. | 12th August - The Haunted Mansion attraction opens at Disneyland in Anaheim, California. Later versions open in Florida, Tokyo and Paris.

22. 15th-18th August - The Woodstock music festival is held on a 600-acre dairy farm in the Catskill Mountains northwest of New York City. Attracting an audience of more than 400,000, many of the most famous musicians of the time turn up and play during the rainy weekend, artists such as; Ravi Shankar, Joan Baez, Santana, Grateful Dead, Creedence Clearwater Revival, Janis Joplin with The Kozmic Blues Band, Sly & the Family Stone, The Who, Jefferson Airplane, Joe Cocker, The Band, Blood Sweat & Tears, Crosby Stills Nash & Young, and Jimi Hendrix. *Fun Fact: Woodstock is widely regarded as a pivotal moment in popular music history and as such, in 2017, the festival site was listed on the U.S. National Register of Historic Places.*

23. | 15th October - Hundreds of thousands of people take part in demonstrations across the United States in the Moratorium to End the War in Vietnam.
24. | 17th October - Willard S. Boyle and George Smith come up with an idea for the first charged-couple device (CCD) at Bell Laboratories in the U.S. *Fun Fact: The CCD became widely used in digital cameras and this invention was recognised with Boyle and Smith being rewarded with a share of the 2009 Nobel Prize in Physics.*
25. | 21st October - Willy Brandt, leader of the Social Democratic Party, becomes Chancellor of West Germany.
26. | 29th October - The first message is sent over ARPANET (the forerunner of the internet) between the University of California, Los Angeles (UCLA) and Stanford Research Institute - it is sent by student programmer Charley Kline.
27. | 15th November - A second Moratorium march in Washington, D.C. sees 500,000 protesters stage a peaceful demonstration against the Vietnam War.
28. | 17th November - Cold War: Negotiators from the Soviet Union and the United States meet in Helsinki to begin the SALT I conferences. Aimed at limiting the number of strategic weapons, an agreement between the two sides is eventually signed on the 26th May 1972.
29. | 19th November - Apollo 12 astronauts Charles Conrad and Alan Bean land at Oceanus Procellarum (Ocean of Storms) to become the third and fourth humans to walk on the Moon. The Command Module Pilot was Richard F. Gordon Jr. who remained in lunar orbit aboard the Yankee Clipper.
30. | 14th December - The Jackson 5 make their first appearance on U.S. televisions iconic Ed Sullivan Show, where a 10 year old Michael Jackson and his 4 brothers dazzle and amaze the audience. The exposure from the show captures the hearts of fans from around the world.

BIRTHS

U.K. PERSONALITIES

BORN IN 1969

Stephen Gordon Hendry, MBE
13th January 1969

Former professional snooker player and current commentator for the BBC and ITV. He is best known for his domination of the sport in the 1990s, during which time he won the World Championship seven times, a record in the modern era. He was also ranked World No.1 for eight consecutive seasons between 1990 and 1998, and again in 2007. The all-time record holder for the number of ranking titles won (36), Hendry is widely regarded as one of the greatest ever snooker players.

James Dean Bradfield
21st February 1969

Singer, songwriter, musician and record producer who is known for being the lead guitarist and lead vocalist for the Welsh alternative rock band Manic Street Preachers. Throughout their career the Manics have headlined several festivals including Glastonbury, T in the Park, V Festival and Reading, and have sold more than ten million albums worldwide. They have also won eleven NME Awards, eight Q Awards and four BRIT Awards.

Lee Alexander McQueen, CBE
17th March 1969 -
11th February 2010

British fashion designer and couturier who founded his own Alexander McQueen label in 1992, and worked as chief designer at Givenchy from 1996 to 2001. His achievements in fashion earned him four British Designer of the Year awards (1996, 1997, 2001 and 2003), as well as the Council of Fashion Designers (CFDA) International Designer of the Year award in 2003. McQueen, who had been diagnosed with mixed anxiety and depressive disorder, committed suicide at his home in Mayfair, London, aged 40.

Karren Rita Brady, Baroness Brady, CBE
4th April 1969

Sporting executive, politician, television personality, newspaper columnist, author and novelist who has featured in the BBC One series The Apprentice since 2010. Known as 'The First Lady of Football' she is the current vice-chairman of West Ham United F.C. Brady has published four books and her latest, Strong Woman, is a Sunday Times Bestseller. On the 22nd September 2014 she was elevated to the House of Lords as a Conservative life peer taking the title Baroness Brady.

Cerys Elizabeth Matthews, MBE
11th April 1969

Singer, songwriter, author, broadcaster and a founding member of Welsh rock band Catatonia. Matthews programmes and hosts a weekly music show on BBC Radio 6 Music, a weekly blues show on BBC Radio 2, and a monthly show on BBC World Service - she also makes documentaries for television and radio, and is a roving reporter for The One Show. She was appointed Member of the Order of the British Empire (MBE) in the 2014 Birthday Honours for her services to music.

Helen Elizabeth 'Tess' Daly
27th April 1969

Model and television presenter best known for co-presenting the BBC One celebrity dancing show Strictly Come Dancing alongside Bruce Forsyth and Claudia Winkleman, and for presenting the BBC telethon Children in Need with Terry Wogan and Fearne Cotton. Daly's career began when she was scouted outside a McDonald's restaurant while waiting for her sister in Manchester (a few weeks before she turned 18). Shortly afterwards she undertook her first professional modelling job in Tokyo.

Darcey Andrea Bussell, DBE
27th April 1969

Retired ballerina and a judge on the BBC reality show Strictly Come Dancing. She trained at the Arts Educational School and the Royal Ballet School, and started her professional career at Sadlers Wells Royal Ballet. In 1989, after only one year, she moved to the Royal Ballet where she became a principal dancer at the age of 20. Bussell remained with The Royal Ballet for her whole career (until her retirement in 2007) and is widely acclaimed as one of the great British ballerinas.

Jacob William Rees-Mogg
24th May 1969

Conservative politician who is the serving Member of Parliament for North East Somerset. He was educated at Eton College and studied History at Trinity College, Oxford where he became President of the Oxford University Conservative Association. After university he worked in the City of London and co-founded the hedge fund management business Somerset Capital Management LLP. Moving into politics he unsuccessfully contested the 1997 and 2001 general elections before being elected as an MP in 2010.

Carys Davina Grey-Thompson, Baroness Grey-Thompson, DBE, DL
26th July 1969

Politician, television presenter and former wheelchair racer better known as Tanni Grey-Thompson. She graduated from Loughborough University in 1991 with a BA (Hons) degree in Politics and Social Administration, and is one of Britain's most successful Paralympic athletes ever. During her athletics career she won a total of 16 Paralympic medals (including 11 golds), held over 30 world records and won the London Marathon six times between 1992 and 2002.

Gary Andrew Speed, MBE
8th September 1969 - 27th November 2011

Professional footballer and manager who played for Leeds United, Everton, Newcastle United, Bolton Wanderers and Sheffield United. Internationally he appeared 85 times for Wales at senior level between 1990 and 2004, a team which he also captained on 44 occasions. Speed was appointed manager of Sheffield United in 2010 only to leave the club after just a few months in December 2010 to manage the Wales national team - he remained in this role until his death 11 months later.

Susan Elizabeth Perkins
22nd September 1969

Comedian, broadcaster, actress and writer who originally came to prominence through her comedy partnership with Mel Giedroyc. She has since become best known as a radio broadcaster and television presenter, most notably of The Great British Bake Off (2010-2016) and Insert Name Here (2016-present). In 2014 Perkins was ranked sixth in The Independent on Sunday's Rainbow List - a list of the most influential openly LGBT individuals in the United Kingdom.

Catherine Zeta-Jones, CBE
25th September 1969

Actress born and raised in Swansea who studied musical theatre at the Arts Educational Schools, London, and made her stage breakthrough with a leading role in a 1987 production of 42nd Street. She went on to find success as a regular in the ITV television series The Darling Buds Of May (1991-1993) before relocating to Los Angeles. Zeta-Jones's move to the U.S. proved successful and she became the recipient of several accolades including an Academy Award, a British Academy Film Award, and a Tony Award.

Polly Jean Harvey, MBE
9th October 1969

Musician, singer-songwriter, writer, poet and composer known as PJ Harvey. In 1991 Harvey formed the PJ Harvey Trio and subsequently began her professional career (the trio released two studio albums before disbanding). After this Harvey continued as a solo artist and since 1995 has released a further nine studio albums. She has received many accolades throughout her career including being the winner of the Mercury Prize in both 2001 and 2011 - the only artist to have been awarded the prize twice.

Steven Rodney McQueen, CBE
9th October 1969

Film director, producer, screenwriter and video artist. For his artwork McQueen received the 1999 Turner Prize, the highest award given to a British visual artist, for his video based on a Buster Keaton film. In 2013 his film 12 Years A Slave won an Academy Award, BAFTA Award, and a Golden Globe Award (he was the first black filmmaker to win an Academy Award for Best Picture). McQueen was awarded the BFI Fellowship in October 2016, the British Film Institute's highest honour.

Gerard James Butler
13th November 1969

Actor and producer. After studying law at the University of Glasgow Butler turned to acting in the mid-1990s with small roles in productions such as Mrs Brown (1997) and the James Bond film Tomorrow Never Dies (1997). It wasn't though until 2007 that Butler gained worldwide recognition for his portrayal of King Leonidas in Zack Snyder's fantasy war film 300. That role earned him the MTV Movie Award for Best Fight, and nominations for an Empire Award and a Saturn Award for Best Actor.

Sajid Javid
5th December 1969

Conservative Party politician and former managing director at Deutsche Bank. He was appointed Home Secretary in April 2018 following Amber Rudd's resignation for misleading the Home Affairs Select Committee over targets for removal of illegal immigrants during the Windrush scandal. He is the first Asian and person from a Muslim background to hold one of the Great Offices of State. Javid has been the Member of Parliament for Bromsgrove in Worcestershire since 2010.

Richard Mark Hammond
19th December 1969

Presenter, writer and journalist best known for co-hosting BBC Two's Top Gear from 2002 until 2015 with Jeremy Clarkson and James May. He has also presented Brainiac: Science Abuse (2003-2008), Total Wipeout (2009-2012) and Planet Earth Live (2012). In 2016 Hammond began presenting The Grand Tour television series with his former Top Gear co-hosts, Clarkson and May, as an exclusive programme distributed via Amazon Video to Amazon Prime customers.

Edward Samuel Miliband
24th December 1969

Politician and former Leader of the Labour Party (2010-2015) who became the Member of Parliament for Doncaster North in 2005. He graduated from Corpus Christi College, Oxford and later from the London School of Economics. Miliband first became a television journalist, then a Labour Party researcher and a visiting scholar at Harvard University, before rising to become one of Chancellor Gordon Brown's confidants. He served in various roles in Prime Minister Gordon Brown's Cabinet from 2007 until Labour's defeat in 2010.

Jay Kay
30th December 1969

Singer-songwriter who was born Jason Luís Cheetham. Kay rose to international fame as a founding member of the jazz-funk band Jamiroquai. After the success of Jamiroquai's first single, When You Gonna Learn, Kay signed a $1 million record deal with Sony Soho2. Whilst under this label the group released a string of million selling albums and singles that have reached various top 10 charts worldwide - to date the band has sold more than 26 million albums worldwide.

NOTABLE BRITISH DEATHS

4th Jan	Daisy and Violet Hilton (b. 5th February 1908) - Entertainers who were conjoined twins. They were exhibited in Europe as children, and toured the U.S. sideshow, vaudeville and burlesque circuits in the 1920s and 1930s. They were best known for their film appearances in Freaks (1932) and Chained For Life (1952).
8th Jan	Albert George Hill (b. 24th March 1889) - Track and field athlete who competed at the 1920 Olympics in Antwerp, Belgium, winning gold medals in both the 800m and 1500m, and a silver medal in the 3000m team race.
11th Jan	Richmal Crompton Lamburn (b. 15th November 1890) - Schoolmistress and popular writer best known for her Just William series of books.
2nd Feb	William Henry Pratt (b. 23rd November 1887) - Actor who is better known by his stage name Boris Karloff, and is primarily remembered for his roles in horror films such as Frankenstein (1931), The Mummy (1932), Bride Of Frankenstein (1935) and Son Of Frankenstein (1939).
14th Feb	Charles Kenneth Horne (b. 27th February 1907) - Comedian and businessman, more commonly known as just Kenneth Horne. He is perhaps best remembered for his work on three BBC Radio series: Much-Binding-In-The-Marsh (1944-1954), Beyond Our Ken (1958-1964), and Round The Horne (1965-1968).
11th Mar	John Wyndham Parkes Lucas Beynon Harris (b. 10th July 1903) - Science fiction writer whose works include The Day Of The Triffids (1951) and The Midwich Cuckoos (1957). Although he often used the pen name John Wyndham, he also used other combinations of his names such as John Beynon and Lucas Parkes.
25th Mar	Alan Mowbray, MM (b. Alfred Ernest Allen; 18th August 1896) - Stage and film actor who found success in Hollywood during 1930s and 1940s. He appeared in over 120 films and was among the founders of the Hollywood Cricket Club.

25th March 1969 - William Edward 'Billy' Cotton (b. 6th May 1899) - Band leader, entertainer, and one of the few whose orchestras survived the British dance band era. Cotton is now mainly remembered as a 1950s and 1960s radio and television personality, but his musical career went as far back as the 1920s. In his younger years Cotton was also an amateur footballer (for Brentford and later for the Athenian league club Wimbledon), an accomplished racing driver, and the owner and pilot of a Gipsy Moth. His autobiography, I Did It My Way, was published posthumously in 1970.

23rd May	Sir Evan Owen Williams (b. 20th March 1890) - An engineer and architect known for being the principal engineer for Gravelly Hill Interchange (Spaghetti Junction), as well as a number of key modernist buildings, including the Express Building in Manchester and Boots D10 Building in Nottingham..

16th Jun | Field Marshal Harold Rupert Leofric George Alexander, 1st Earl Alexander of Tunis, KG, GCB, OM, GCMG, CSI, DSO, MC, CD, PC (b. 10th December 1891) - A senior British Army officer who served with distinction in both the First and Second World Wars and, afterwards, as Governor General of Canada.

3rd July 1969 - Brian Jones (b. Lewis Brian Hopkin Jones; 28th February 1942) - Musician who founded and was the original leader of the Rolling Stones. Initially a slide guitarist, Jones would go on to play a wide variety of instruments on Rolling Stones recordings and in concerts; instruments such as rhythm and lead guitar, piano, organ, marimba, harmonica, sitar, recorder, saxophone and oboe amongst others. Andrew Loog Oldham's arrival as manager of the Stones marked the beginning of Jones' slow estrangement. Oldham pushed the band into a musical direction at odds with Jones's blues background. Around the same time Jones developed a drug problem and his performance in the studio became increasingly unreliable, leading to a diminished role within the band he founded. The Rolling Stones asked Jones to leave in June 1969 and guitarist Mick Taylor took his place in the group. Jones died less than a month later after drowning in his swimming pool whilst under the influence of drugs.

14th Jul | Henry Wale (b. 14th July 1891) - Stage and film actor known professionally as Henry Oscar.

9th Aug | Cecil Frank Powell, FRS (b. 5th December 1903) - Physicist who won the Nobel Prize in Physics for his 'development of the photographic method of studying nuclear processes and for the resulting discovery of the pion (pi-meson), a subatomic particle'.

14th Aug | Leonard Sidney Woolf (b. 25th November 1880) - Political theorist, author, publisher and civil servant who was married to author Virginia Woolf.

27th Aug | Dame Ivy Compton-Burnett, DBE (b. 5th June 1884) - Novelist who was awarded the 1955 James Tait Black Memorial Prize for her novel Mother and Son. Her works consist mainly of dialogue and focus on family life among the late Victorian and Edwardian upper middle class. Manservant and Maidservant (1947) is considered one of her best.

18th Nov | George Edward 'Ted' Heath (b. 30th March 1902) - Musician and big band leader who led Britain's greatest post-war big band. The band recorded more than 100 albums altogether, selling over 20 million copies.

5th Dec | Princess Alice of Battenberg (b. Victoria Alice Elizabeth Julia Marie; 25th February 1885) - The mother of Prince Philip, Duke of Edinburgh, and mother-in-law of Queen Elizabeth II.

7th Dec | Hugh Williams (b. Hugh Anthony Glanmore Williams; 6th March 1904) - Actor, playwright and dramatist of Welsh descent.

1969 TOP 10 SINGLES

Archies	No.1	Sugar Sugar
Rolling Stones	No.2	Honky Tonk Women
Fleetwood Mac	No.3	Albatross
Beatles w/ Billy Preston	No.4	Get Back
Marvin Gaye	No.5	I Heard It Through The Grapevine
Jane Birkin & Serge Gainsbourg	No.6	Je T'aime... Moi Non Plus
Bobbie Gentry	No.7	I'll Never Fall In Love Again
Peter Sarstedt	No.8	Where Do You Go To (My Lovely)?
Zager & Evans	No.9	In The Year 2525
Creedence Clearwater Revival	No.10	Bad Moon Rising

N.B. This chart has been compiled from official data, using a combination of weeks spent at the No.1 spot and length of time charting in the Top 10, to determine the most popular songs released between the 1st Jan and 31st Dec 1969.

Archies
Sugar Sugar

Label:	Written by:	Length:
RCA Victor	Andy Kim / Jeff Barry	2 mins 48 secs

The Archies were a fictional garage band founded by Archie Andrews, Reggie Mantle, Jughead Jones, Veronica Lodge and Betty Cooper, a group of adolescent characters from the animated American TV series The Archie Show. The fictional band's music was recorded by session musicians and featured vocalists Ron Dante and Toni Wine. Sugar, Sugar was The Archies most successful song and became one of the biggest hits of the bubble-gum pop genre that flourished from 1968 to 1973.

Rolling Stones
Honky Tonk Women

Label:	Written by:	Length:
Decca	Jagger / Richards	3 mins 0 secs

The Rolling Stones were formed in London in 1962 and the line-up at the time Honky Tonk Women was released was Mick Jagger (lead vocals), Keith Richards (guitar, backing vocals), Mick Taylor (lead guitar), Bill Wyman (bass) and Charlie Watts (drums). They have to date released 30 studio, 23 live and numerous compilations albums, and have estimated total record sales in excess of 250 million units.

3 Fleetwood Mac
Albatross

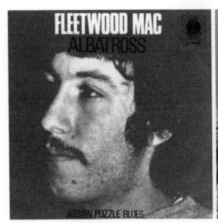 

Label:	Written by:	Length:
Blue Horizon	Peter Green	3 mins 0 secs

Fleetwood Mac are a British-American rock band formed in London in 1967. The group has sold more than 100 million records worldwide making them one of the world's best-selling bands. Albatross, a guitar-based instrumental, was a major hit in several countries and became Fleetwood Mac's only No.1 hit in the UK. In 1998 select members of Fleetwood Mac were inducted into the Rock and Roll Hall of Fame and also became the recipients of the Brit Award for Outstanding Contribution to Music.

4 Beatles w/ Billy Preston
Get Back

Label:	Written by:	Length:
Apple Records	Lennon / McCartney	3 mins 8 secs

The Beatles were formed in Liverpool in 1960 and are widely regarded as the greatest and most influential act of the rock era. They are the best-selling band in history with estimated sales of over 600 million records worldwide and have received ten Grammy Awards, an Academy Award and fifteen Ivor Novello Awards. The group was inducted into the Rock and Roll Hall of Fame in 1988.

Marvin Gaye
I Heard It Through The Grapevine

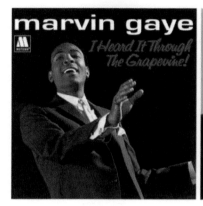  

Label:	Written by:	Length:
Tamla	Strong / Whitfield	2 mins 59 secs

Marvin Pentz Gaye (b. 2nd April 1939 - d. 1st April 1984) was an American singer, songwriter and record producer. Gaye helped to shape the sound of Motown in the 1960s, first as an in-house session player and later as a solo artist, and had a string of hits which included the soul classic 'I Heard It Through The Grapevine'. Since his death he has been bestowed with many awards, including a Grammy Lifetime Achievement Award, and has been inducted in to the Rhythm and Blues, Songwriters and Rock and Roll Halls of Fame.

Jane Birkin & Serge Gainsbourg
Je T'aime... Moi Non Plus

Label:	Written by:	Length:
Fontana	Serge Gainsbourg	4 mins 25 secs

Jane Mallory Birkin, OBE (b. 14th December 1946) is an actress, singer, songwriter and model who attained international fame and notability for her decade-long musical and romantic partnership with Serge Gainsbourg. Originally written by Gainsbourg for Brigitte Bardot in 1967, Je T'aime... Moi Non Plus (French for I love you... neither do I) reached the No.1 spot in the UK and No.2 in Ireland - it was banned in several other countries due to its overly sexual content.

7 Bobbie Gentry
I'll Never Fall In Love Again

Label:	Written by:	Length:
Capitol Records	Bacharach / David	2 mins 50 secs

Bobbie Lee Gentry (b. Roberta Lee Streeter; 27th July 1942) is an American singer-songwriter who was one of the first female artists to compose and produce her own material. Gentry rose to international fame with her intriguing Southern Gothic narrative 'Ode To Billie Joe' in 1967. I'll Never Fall In Love Again, by composer Burt Bacharach and lyricist Hal David, was written for the 1968 musical Promises, Promises and was Gentrys only UK No.1 recording.

---

8 Peter Sarstedt
Where Do You Go To (My Lovely)?

Label:	Written by:	Length:
United Artists Records	Peter Sarstedt	4 mins 36 secs

Peter Eardley Sarstedt (b. 10th December 1941 - d. 8th January 2017), briefly billed early in his career as Peter Lincoln, was a singer, instrumentalist and songwriter. He was best known for writing and performing the single 'Where Do You Go To (My Lovely)?' which went on to win an Ivor Novello Award. The recording remained Sarstedt's biggest hit despite him releasing numerous other successful albums and singles from the late 1960s onwards.

Zager & Evans
In The Year 2525

Label:	Written by:	Length:
RCA Victor	Rick Evans	3 mins 15 secs

Zager and Evans were a rock-pop duo named after its two members, Denny Zager (b. 14th February 1944) and Rick Evans (b. 20th January 1943). They are best known for their single In The Year 2525, and remain the only artist to have had a chart-topping record on both sides of the Atlantic and never have another hit single. To date In The Year 2525 is also the biggest ever one-hit wonder of any artist, at any time in recording history, selling over 20 million records worldwide.

Creedence Clearwater Revival
Bad Moon Rising

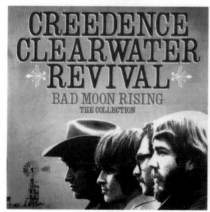 

Label:	Written by:	Length:
Liberty	John Fogerty	2 mins 17 secs

Creedence Clearwater Revival (often referred to as Creedence or CCR) was an American rock band active in the late 1960s and early 1970s which consisted of lead vocalist, lead guitarist, and primary songwriter John Fogerty, his brother rhythm guitarist Tom Fogerty, bassist Stu Cook and drummer Doug Clifford. Bad Moon Rising was the lead single from their album Green River and was their biggest charting hit in the UK.

1969: TOP FILMS

1. **Butch Cassidy And The Sundance Kid** - *20th Century Fox*
2. **Midnight Cowboy** - *United Artists*
3. **Easy Rider** - *Columbia*
4. **Hello, Dolly!** - *20th Century Fox*
5. **Bob & Carol & Ted & Alice** - *Columbia*

OSCARS

Best Picture: Midnight Cowboy

Most Nominations: Anne Of The Thousand Days (10)
Most Wins: Butch Cassidy And The Sundance Kid (4)

Best Director: John Schlesinger - *Midnight Cowboy*

Best Actor: John Wayne - *True Grit*
Best Actress: Maggie Smith - *The Prime Of Miss Jean Brodie*
Best Supporting Actor: Gig Young - *They Shoot Horses, Don't They?*
Best Supporting Actress: Goldie Hawn - *Cactus Flower*

The 42nd Academy Awards were presented on the 7th April, 1970.

BUTCH CASSIDY AND THE SUNDANCE KID

Directed by: George Roy Hill - Runtime: 1 hour 50 minutes

Butch Cassidy and The Sundance Kid are the leaders of a band of outlaws in Wyoming in the early 1900s. After a train robbery goes wrong they find themselves on the run with a posse hard on their heels. Their solution - escape to Bolivia.

STARRING

Paul Newman
Born: 26th January 1925
Died: 26th September 2008

Character:
Butch Cassidy

Paul Leonard Newman was an American actor, IndyCar driver, entrepreneur, activist, and philanthropist. He won numerous acting awards including an Oscar for his role in the 1986 film The Color Of Money. He starred in many other classic films including The Hustler (1961), Cool Hand Luke (1967) and The Sting (1973). Newman co-founded food company Newman's Own which has so far donated over US$485 million to charity.

Robert Redford
Born: 18th August 1936

Character:
The Sundance Kid

Actor, director, producer, businessman, environmentalist, philanthropist and the founder of the Sundance Film Festival. He made his film debut in 1962 but it was his role in Butch Cassidy And The Sundance Kid which made him a major star. He has received two Academy Awards: one in 1981 for directing Ordinary People and one for Lifetime Achievement in 2002. In 2016 Redford was honoured with the U.S. Presidential Medal of Freedom.

Katharine Ross
Born: 29th January 1940

Character:
Etta Place

Katharine Juliet Ross is an American film and stage actress. She had starring roles in three of the most popular films of the 1960s and 1970s: as Elaine Robinson in The Graduate (1967), for which she received a nomination for the Academy Award for Best Supporting Actress; as Etta Place in Butch Cassidy And The Sundance Kid, for which she won a BAFTA Award for Best Actress; and as Joanna Eberhart in The Stepford Wives (1975).

TRIVIA

Goofs In the opening sequence, when Sundance shoots the gun belt off the card player, the film has been cut to make the quick draw appear faster - you can see Butch Cassidy's image jump across the screen in the background.

The foot-pegs through the front axle of the bicycle that Etta uses disappear during Butch Cassidy's stunt performance and reappear afterwards.

Interesting Facts With nine wins the film currently holds the record for the most British Academy Awards (BAFTAs).

CONTINUED

Interesting Facts

The real Butch Cassidy, whose name was actually Robert Leroy Parker, got his nickname because he once worked in a butcher's shop. The Sundance Kid, real name Harry Alonzo Longabaugh, got his nickname because he once was arrested in the Wyoming town of Sundance.

Robert Redford wanted to do all of his own stunts. Paul Newman was especially upset about Redford's desire to jump onto the train roof and run along the tops of the carriages as it moved. Redford said Newman told him, "I don't want any heroics around here. I don't want to lose a co-star."

Katharine Ross enjoyed shooting the silent bicycle riding sequence best because it was handled by the film crew's Second Unit rather than the director. She said, "Any day away from George Roy Hill was a good one".

The bull's name in the film is Bill. He was flown in from Los Angeles for the bicycle scene, which was shot in Utah. In order to make Bill charge a substance was sprayed on his testicles. Oddly he didn't seem to mind and endured it through several takes.

The Writers Guild of America ranked the screenplay number eleven on its list of the 101 Greatest Screenplays ever written.

Quotes

Butch Cassidy: Do you believe I'm broke already?
Etta Place: Why is there never any money, Butch?
Butch Cassidy: Well, I swear, Etta, I don't know. I've been working like a dog all my life and I can't get a penny ahead.
Etta Place: Sundance says it's because you're a soft touch, and always taking expensive vacations, and buying drinks for everyone, and you're a rotten gambler.
Butch Cassidy: Well that might have something to do with it.

Butch Cassidy: Kid, there's something I ought to tell you. I never shot anybody before.
Sundance Kid: One hell of a time to tell me!

MIDNIGHT COWBOY

1989 **BEST** PICTURE DIRECTOR SCREENPLAY ADAPTATION

A JEROME HELLMAN-JOHN SCHLESINGER PRODUCTION

DUSTIN HOFFMAN
JON VOIGHT
"MIDNIGHT COWBOY"

Directed by: John Schlesinger - Runtime: 1 hour 53 minutes

Naive hustler Joe Buck travels from Texas to New York City to seek personal fortune and finds a new friend in crook Enrico Salvatore 'Ratso' Rizzo.

STARRING

Dustin Hoffman
Born: 8th August 1937

Character:
Ratso Rizzo

Actor and director with a career in film, television and theatre since 1960. He has been known for his versatile portrayals of antiheroes and vulnerable characters. Hoffman has been nominated for seven Academy Awards, winning twice for Best Actor in Kramer vs. Kramer (1979), and Rain Man (1988). He has also won six Golden Globes (including an honorary one) and four BAFTAs.

Jon Voight
Born: 29th December 1938

Character:
Joe Buck

Jonathan Vincent Voight is an actor who first came to prominence in Midnight Cowboy with his Oscar nominated performance as would-be gigolo Joe Buck. During the 1970s he became a Hollywood star with his portrayals of a businessman mixed up with murder in Deliverance (1972); a paraplegic Vietnam veteran in Coming Home (1978), for which he won an Academy Award for Best Actor; and a penniless ex-boxing champion in the remake of The Champ (1979).

Sylvia Miles
Born: 9th September 1924

Character:
Cass

Film, stage, and television actress whose career started in 1960 playing the role of Sadie in the film Murder, Inc. She has been nominated twice for the Academy Award for Best Supporting Actress for her performances as an aging Park Avenue kept-woman in Midnight Cowboy, despite only appearing on-screen for about six minutes, and for her slightly larger role (eight minutes) as Jessie Halstead Florian in Farewell, My Lovely (1975).

TRIVIA

Goofs | After Joe Buck's encounter with Towny he and Ratso board the bus to Miami. The bus then enters the south tube of the Lincoln Tunnel which only carries eastbound traffic into New York.

A ceilingless set and lighting equipment can be briefly seen in several shots in Cass' bedroom.

Interesting Facts | Jon Voight was paid the Screen Actors Guild minimum wage for his portrayal of Joe Buck, a concession he willingly made to obtain the part.

CONTINUED

Interesting Facts

Before Dustin Hoffman auditioned for this film he knew that his all-American image could easily cost him the job. To prove he could do it he asked the auditioning film executive to meet him on a street corner in Manhattan, and in the meantime, dressed himself in filthy rags. The executive arrived at the appointed corner and waited, barely noticing Hoffman dressed as a "beggar" less than ten feet away accosting people for spare change. Eventually Hoffman walked up to him and revealed his true identity.

On the occasion of the film's 25th anniversary in 1994, Hoffman revealed on Larry King Live that when the movie was first previewed the audience started to leave in droves during gay encounter scene between Jon Voight and Bob Balaban.

The film was banned in Ireland by the Irish Film Censorship Board in September 1969. It did eventually receive a theatrical release in Ireland in 1971 when it was passed with an 18 certificate by the Irish Film Appeals Board.

Dustin Hoffman spent a considerable amount of time in the New York City slums observing tramps and studying their physical movements and behaviour.

Warren Beatty was interested in playing Joe Buck but John Schlesinger thought he was too famous to be believable as a naive street hustler.

Quotes

Ratso Rizzo: You know, in my own place, my name ain't Ratso. I mean, it just so happens that in my own place my name is Enrico Salvatore Rizzo.
Joe Buck: Well, I can't say all that.
Ratso Rizzo: Rico, then.

Ratso Rizzo: Come on man, don't hit me. Come on, man. Come on, I'm a cripple!
Joe Buck: I ain't gonna hit you!
Ratso Rizzo: Come on...
Joe Buck: I'm gonna STRANGLE you to death!

Ratso Rizzo: I'm walking here! I'm walking here!

EASY RIDER

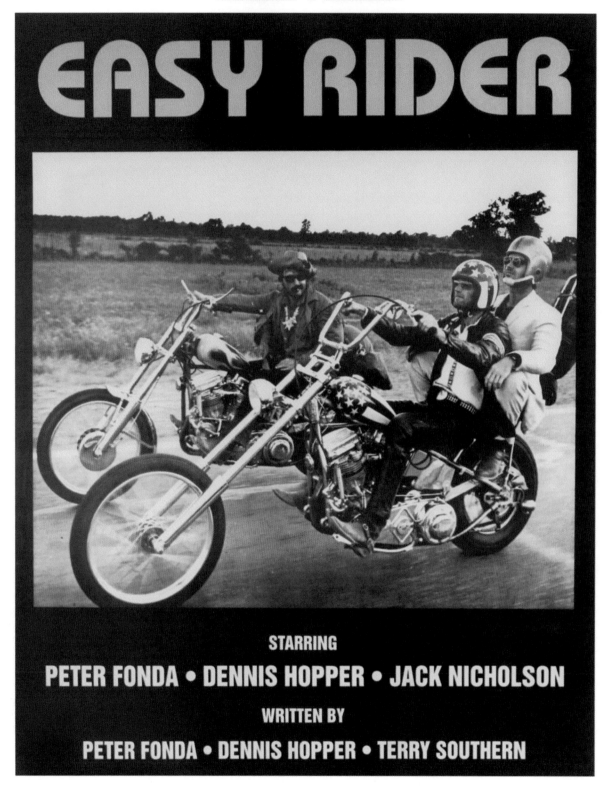

EASY RIDER

STARRING

PETER FONDA • DENNIS HOPPER • JACK NICHOLSON

WRITTEN BY

PETER FONDA • DENNIS HOPPER • TERRY SOUTHERN

Directed by: Dennis Hopper - Runtime: 1 hour 35 minutes

Two bikers head from L.A to New Orleans and along the way meet a man who bridges a counter-culture gap they are unaware of.

STARRING

Peter Fonda
Born: 23rd February 1940

Character:
Wyatt

Actor who made his professional stage debut on Broadway in 1961 in Blood, Sweat And Stanley Poole, for which he received rave reviews from the New York Critics, won the Daniel Blum Theater World Award and the New York Critics Circle Award for Best New Actor. He has been nominated twice for an Academy Award, once for Best Original Screenplay for Easy Rider (1969), and again for Best Actor in Ulee's Gold (1997).

Dennis Hopper
Born: 17th May 1936
Died: 29th May 2010

Characters:
Billy

Actor, director, writer, film editor, photographer and artist. He made his first television appearance in 1954 and soon after appeared alongside James Dean in the film Rebel Without A Cause (1955). In the next ten years he made a name in television and by the end of the 1960s had appeared in several films. Hopper also began a prolific and acclaimed photography career in the 1960s, and in 1969 also made his directorial film debut with Easy Rider.

Jack Nicholson
Born: 22nd April 1937

Character:
George Hanson

John Joseph Nicholson is an actor and filmmaker who has performed for over sixty years. His 12 Academy Award nominations make him the most nominated male actor in the Academy's history and he is one of only three male actors to win three Oscars; he won an Academy Award for Best Actor for his roles in One Flew Over The Cuckoo's Nest (1975) and for As Good As It Gets (1997), and for Best Supporting Actor in Terms Of Endearment (1983).

TRIVIA

Goofs | In one of the riding across the bridge montage scenes you can see the camera man filming from the trunk of a car in the reflection of Wyatt's sunglasses.

The scene just before Wyatt throws away his watch is a mirror image. The bike appears to be leaning to the right on the kickstand (instead of the left) and his jacket has stripes down the right side but in the rest of the movie they're down the left side.

Interesting Facts | Peter Fonda, Dennis Hopper and Jack Nicholson were actually smoking marijuana on camera. LSD, however, was not actually used during the acid scene.

CONTINUED

Interesting Facts Dennis Hopper and Peter Fonda did not write a full script for the movie and made most of it up as they went along. They didn't hire a crew but instead picked up hippies at communes across the country and used friends and passers-by to hold the cameras.

Easy Rider was one of the first films to make extensive use of previously released musical tracks rather than a specially written film score. This is common with films now but was quite unusual at the time.

Some of the weird lighting effects in the LSD scene came about because a can of film was accidentally exposed when it was opened before being developed.

According to Peter Fonda four police bikes were customised for the film. One was burned during filming and the other three were stolen before filming was completed.

Karen Black described the shoot as "insane". According to Jack Nicholson, "Everyone wanted to kill one another and put one another in institutions".

Quotes **Wyatt:** *[reading inscription]* If god did not exist it would be necessary to invent him.
Billy: That's a humdinger!

George Hanson: *[Drinking his Jim Beam]* Here's the first of the day fellas! To old D.H. Lawrence.
[He starts flapping one arm like a chicken]
George Hanson: Neh! Neh! Neh! Fuh! Fuh! Fuh! Indians.

HELLO, DOLLY!

20th CENTURY-FOX PRESENTS

BARBRA STREISAND — **WALTER MATTHAU** / **MICHAEL CRAWFORD**

IN
ERNEST LEHMAN'S PRODUCTION OF
HELLO, DOLLY!

AND
LOUIS ARMSTRONG

WRITTEN FOR THE SCREEN
AND PRODUCED BY
ERNEST LEHMAN

DIRECTED BY
GENE KELLY

ASSOCIATE PRODUCER
ROGER EDENS

DANCES AND
MUSICAL NUMBERS
STAGED BY
MICHAEL KIDD

MUSIC AND LYRICS BY
JERRY HERMAN

Directed by: Gene Kelly - Runtime: 2 hours 26 minutes

In 1890s New York City the bold and enchanting widow Dolly Levi is a socialite-turned-matchmaker. The film follows her exploits as she travels to Yonkers to find a match for the miserly 'well-known unmarried half-a-millionaire' Horace Vandergelder.

44

STARRING

Barbra Streisand
Born: 24th April 1942

Character:
Dolly Levi

Singer, songwriter, actress and filmmaker. During a career spanning six decades she has become an icon in multiple fields of entertainment winning two Academy Awards - for Funny Girl (1968) and A Star Is Born (1976) - ten Grammys, five Emmys, a Special Tony Award, an American Film Institute Award, a Kennedy Center Honors prize, four Peabody Awards and nine Golden Globes. In 2015 she was awarded the Presidential Medal of Freedom by Barack Obama.

Walter Matthau
Born: 1st October 1920
Died: 1st July 2000

Character:
Horace Vandergelder

Actor and comedian best known for his role as Oscar Madison in The Odd Couple and his frequent collaborations with Odd Couple co-star Jack Lemmon (particularly in the 1990's with Grumpy Old Men and its sequel Grumpier Old Men). Matthau won the Academy Award for Best Supporting Actor for his performance in the Billy Wilder film The Fortune Cookie (1966), and was also the winner of two BAFTA's, a Golden Globe and two Tony awards.

Michael Crawford
Born: 19th January 1942

Character:
Cornelius Hackl

Actor, comedian, singer, voice artist and philanthropist born Michael Patrick Smith. Crawford has received international critical acclaim and won numerous awards during his career, which has included many film and television performances as well as stagework on both London's West End and on Broadway in New York City. He is probably best known for playing the character Frank Spencer in the popular 1970s sitcom Some Mothers Do 'Ave 'Em and for originating the title role in The Phantom Of The Opera.

TRIVIA

Goofs | Although the film is set in 1890 modern electrical power transformers are visible on the utility poles in the Yonkers scenes.

The red-carpeted staircase at the Harmonia Gardens restaurant has brass carpet rods on each stair during all of the scenes prior to the arrival of Dolly Levi. When she arrives and they sing 'Hello, Dolly!' the carpet rods are gone.

Interesting Facts | Gene Kelly fought to keep Michael Crawford's singing voice, which the producers wanted to dub.

CONTINUED

Interesting Facts

Barbra Streisand and Walter Matthau fought bitterly during filming. He disliked her so intensely that he refused to be around her unless the script required it. He is famously quoted as telling Streisand that she "had no more talent than a butterfly's fart".

On a break from filming, Walter Matthau and Michael Crawford visited a nearby racetrack and saw a horse named Hello Dolly. Matthau refused to place a bet on it because it reminded him of Barbra Streisand. Crawford placed a bet on the horse. It won the race and Matthau refused to speak to Crawford for the rest of the shoot unless absolutely necessary.

This was the very first film released on home video (VHS and Betamax) in the U.S. It was released in Autumn 1977 by the Magnetic Video Corporation, the first of the 50 original films it licensed from Fox. Its catalogue number was CL-1001.

In the Harmonia Gardens, the back wall behind the hat-check girl is the wall from the ballroom of the Von Trapps Villa in The Sound of Music (1965).

Hello, Dolly! was the most expensive musical ever produced at the time of the film's release.

Quotes

Dolly Levi: Money, pardon the expression, is like manure. It's not worth a thing unless it's spread around, encouraging young things to grow.

Horace Vandergelder: Eighty percent of the people in the world are fools and the rest of us are in danger of contamination.

BOB & CAROL & TED & ALICE

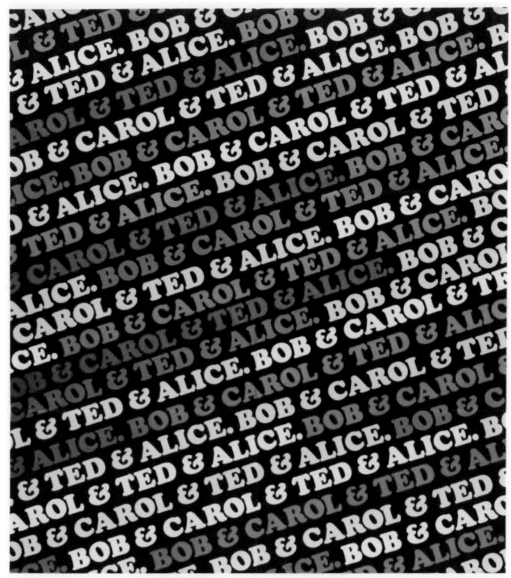

consider the possibilities

COLUMBIA PICTURES presents
A FRANKOVICH PRODUCTION

NATALIE WOOD   ROBERT CULP

BOB & CAROL & TED & ALICE

ELLIOTT GOULD   DYAN CANNON

Directed by: Paul Mazursky - Runtime: 1 hour 45 minutes

After a weekend of emotional honesty at an Esalen-style retreat, Los Angeles sophisticates Bob and Carol Sanders return home determined to embrace complete openness. The couple then proceed share their enthusiasm and excitement over their new-found philosophy with their more conservative friends Ted and Alice Henderson.

STARRING

Natalie Wood
Born: 20th July 1938
Died: 29th November 1981

Character:
Carol Sanders

Russian-American actress born Natalia Nikolaevna Zakharenko. Wood began her career in film as a child and became a successful Hollywood star as a young adult, receiving three Academy Award nominations before she turned 25 years old. Notable films include Miracle On 34th Street (1947), Rebel Without A Cause (1955), West Side Story (1961), Gypsy (1962), Splendor In The Grass (1961) and Love With The Proper Stranger (1963).

Robert Culp
Born: 16th August 1930
Died: 24th March 2010

Character:
Bob Sanders

An actor, screenwriter, voice actor, and director, widely known for his work in television in a career spanning more than 50 years. Culp earned an international reputation for his role as Kelly Robinson on I Spy (1965-1968) and worked as an actor in many theatrical films, beginning with three in 1963; PT 109, The Raiders, and Sunday In New York. The 1980s brought him back to television starring in The Greatest American Hero, and Everybody Loves Raymond.

Elliott Gould
Born: 29th August 1938

Characters:
Ted Henderson

Actor born Elliott Goldstein who began acting in Hollywood films during the 1960s. Gould is perhaps best known for his significant leading roles in Robert Altman films; starring in M*A*S*H (1970), The Long Goodbye (1973), and California Split (1974). More recently he has gained recognition for his recurring supporting roles as Jack Geller on Friends (1994-2004), as Reuben Tishkoff in the Ocean's Trilogy (2001-2007), and as Ezra Goldman in Ray Donovan (2013-2015).

TRIVIA

Goofs	In the restaurant kitchen Carol takes hold of the waiter's left hand but in the next shot she is holding his right hand. The camera crew's reflections are visible during the opening helicopter shots.
Interesting Facts	Natalie Wood decided to gamble her standard fee on a percentage of the gross. This earned her $3 million and averted her making the same mistake she did when she declined a similar offer with West Side Story (1961).

CONTINUED

Interesting Facts | This was Natalie Wood's first film since starring in Penelope (1966). She would not star in another movie for four years when she would co-star in The Affair (1973) with her first husband Robert Wagner (with whom she had recently remarried).

Donald F. Muhich who played Alice Henderson's therapist was director Paul Mazursky's real-life therapist. He later appeared in three other Mazursky films.

Actors who turned down roles in the film included Warren Beatty, Robert Redford, Steve McQueen, Tuesday Weld, Jane Fonda and Faye Dunaway.

Quotes | **Alice Henderson:** You know how children are, they're very curious. He wanted to know why I had a tee-tee...
Psychiatrist: Pardon me? I don't know what a tee-tee is.
Alice Henderson: A vagina.
Psychiatrist: Oh, it's a pet expression of yours.
Alice Henderson: Yes, you know words: tee-tee, tinkle, po-po, wee-wee, kee-kee, poo-poo.
Psychiatrist: I had never heard tee-tee before.
Alice Henderson: What expression do you use with your children?
Psychiatrist: Vagina.

SPORTING WINNERS

B B C SPORTS PERSONALITY OF THE YEAR

ANN JONES - TENNIS

Ann Shirley Jones, CBE (née Adrianne Haydon; 7th October 1938) is a former table tennis and lawn tennis champion. She won a total of 8 Grand Slam championships throughout her career and reached a career high of World No.2 in both 1967 and 1969.

Grand Slam Titles:

	Singles	Doubles	Mixed Doubles
Australian Open	-	-	1969
French Open	1961 / 1966	1963 / 1968 / 1969	-
Wimbledon	1969	-	-
U.S. Open	-	-	1969

In 1985 Jones was voted into the International Tennis Hall of Fame. For many years she was chairwoman of the International Women's Tennis Council and has long been a member of Wimbledon's Committee of Management. Jones became the first ever 'civilian woman' (i.e. not a member of the British Royal Family) to present the trophies at Wimbledon when she awarded the winners of the Mixed Doubles championship their cup in 2007, a ceremony she now regularly performs.

FIVE NATIONS RUGBY
WINNERS - WALES

Position	Nation	Played	Won	Draw	Lost	For	Against	+/-	Points
1st	**Wales**	**4**	**3**	**1**	**0**	**79**	**31**	**+48**	**7**
2nd	Ireland	4	3	0	1	61	48	+13	6
3rd	England	4	2	0	2	54	58	-4	4
4th	Scotland	4	1	0	3	12	44	-34	2
5th	France	4	0	1	3	28	53	-25	1

The 1969 Five Nations Championship was the fortieth series of the rugby union Five Nations Championship. Including the previous incarnations as the Home Nations and Five Nations, this was the seventy-fifth series of the northern hemisphere rugby union championship. Ten matches were played between the 11th January and 12th April with Wales winning its 16th title (missing out on the Grand Slam due to a draw with France, but taking home the Triple Crown).

Date	Team		Score		Team	Location
11-01-1969	France	▮▮	3-6	⊠	Scotland	Stade Olympique, Paris
25-01-1969	Ireland		17-9	▮▮	France	Lansdowne Road, Dublin
01-02-1969	Scotland	⊠	3-17		Wales	Murrayfield, Edinburgh
08-02-1969	Ireland		17-15	✛	England	Lansdowne Road, Dublin
22-02-1969	England	✛	22-8	▮▮	France	Twickenham, London
22-02-1969	Scotland	⊠	0-16		Ireland	Murrayfield, Edinburgh
08-03-1969	Wales		24-11		Ireland	National Stadium, Cardiff
15-03-1969	England	✛	8-3	⊠	Scotland	Twickenham, London
22-03-1969	France	▮▮	8-8		Wales	Stade Olympique, Paris
12-04-1969	Wales		30-9	✛	England	National Stadium, Cardiff

CALCUTTA CUP

ENGLAND ✛ 8-3 ⊠ SCOTLAND

The Calcutta Cup was first awarded in 1879 and is the rugby union trophy awarded to the winner of the match (currently played as part of the Six Nations Championship) between England and Scotland. The Cup was presented to the Rugby Football Union after the Calcutta Football Club in India disbanded in 1878. It is made from melted down silver rupees withdrawn from the clubs funds.

Historical Records	England	Scotland	Draws
	70 Wins	40 Wins	15

BRITISH GRAND PRIX - JACKIE STEWART

Jackie Stewart takes the British Grand Prix at Silverstone.

The 1969 British Grand Prix was held at the Silverstone Circuit on the 19th July. It was race 6 of 11 in both the 1969 World Championship of Drivers and the 1969 International Cup for Formula One Manufacturers. Jackie Stewart was victorious after lapping the entire field and taking his fifth win in six races.

Pos.	Country	Driver	Constructor
1st	**United Kingdom**	**Jackie Stewart**	**Matra-Ford**
2nd	Belgium	Jacky Ickx	Brabham-Ford
3rd	New Zealand	Bruce McLaren	McLaren-Ford

1969 GRAND PRIX SEASON

Rnd	Date	Race	Winning Driver	Constructor
1	1st Mar	South African Grand Prix	Jackie Stewart	Matra-Ford
2	4th May	Spanish Grand Prix	Jackie Stewart	Matra-Ford
3	18th May	Monaco Grand Prix	Graham Hill	Lotus-Ford
4	21st Jun	Dutch Grand Prix	Jackie Stewart	Matra-Ford
5	6th Jul	French Grand Prix	Jackie Stewart	Matra-Ford
6	19th Jul	British Grand Prix	Jackie Stewart	Matra-Ford
7	3rd Aug	German Grand Prix	Jacky Ickx	Brabham-Ford
8	7th Sep	Italian Grand Prix	Jackie Stewart	Matra-Ford
9	20th Sep	Canadian Grand Prix	Jacky Ickx	Brabham-Ford
10	5th Oct	United States Grand Prix	Jochen Rindt	Lotus-Ford
11	19th Oct	Mexican Grand Prix	Denny Hulme	McLaren-Ford

The 1969 Formula One season was the 23rd season of FIA Formula One motor racing and concluded with Jackie Stewart taking the Drivers' Championship title with 63 points. Second and third places went to Jacky Ickx and Bruce McLaren with 37 and 26 points respectively.

GRAND NATIONAL - HIGHLAND WEDDING

The 1969 Grand National was the 123rd renewal of this world famous horse race and took place at Aintree Racecourse near Liverpool on the 29th March. Twelve-year-old Highland Wedding, running in his third Grand National and ridden by jockey Eddie Harty, was the winner by 12 lengths.

Thirty horses contested the 1969 Grand National; 14 horses completed the course, 9 fell, 3 refused, 3 pulled up and 1 was brought down. The 13/2 favourite Red Alligator fell at the 19th fence.

Pos.	Name	Jockey	Age	Weight	Odds
1st	**Highland Wedding**	**Eddie Harty**	**12**	**10st-4lb**	**100/9**
2nd	Steel Bridge	Richard Pitman	11	10st-0lb	50/1
3rd	Rondetto	Jeff King	13	10st-6lb	25/1
4th	The Beeches	Bill Rees	9	10st-1lb	100/6

GOLF OPEN CHAMPIONSHIP - TONY JACKLIN

Tony Jacklin wins the 1969 Open and Claret Jug.

The 1969 Open Championship was the 98th to be played and was held between the 9th and 12th of July at the Royal Lytham & St Annes Golf Club in Lytham St Annes, England. Tony Jacklin won the first of his two major championships, two strokes ahead of New Zealander Bob Charles, and became the first Briton to win The Open since 1951. In total 130 players took part in the competition; Jacklin's share of the £30,000 prize fund was £4,250.

FOOTBALL LEAGUE CHAMPIONS

England:

Pos.	Team	W	D	L	F	A	Pts.
1st	**Leeds United**	**27**	**13**	**2**	**66**	**26**	**67**
2nd	Liverpool	25	11	6	63	24	61
3rd	Everton	21	15	6	77	36	57
4th	Arsenal	22	12	8	56	27	56
5th	Chelsea	20	10	12	73	53	50

Scotland:

Pos.	Team	W	D	L	F	A	Pts.
1st	**Celtic**	**23**	**8**	**3**	**89**	**32**	**54**
2nd	Rangers	21	7	6	81	32	49
3rd	Dunfermline Athletic	19	7	8	63	45	45
4th	Kilmarnock	15	14	5	50	32	44
5th	Dundee United	17	9	8	61	49	43

FA CUP WINNERS - MANCHESTER CITY

Manchester City captain Tony Book and his team mates celebrate after winning the Cup.

Manchester City   1-0   Leicester City
Young ⚽ 24'

Referee: George McCabe (South Yorkshire)

The 1969 FA Cup Final took place on the 26th April at Wembley Stadium in front of 100,000 fans. This was the first FA Cup final since 1951 to take place in the month of April. Three-time winners Manchester City were appearing in their seventh final, whereas Leicester City were seeking to win the competition for the first time, having lost three previous finals.

WIMBLEDON

Ann Jones and Rod Laver winning their respective Wimbledon Championship titles.

Men's Singles Champion - Rod Laver - Australia
Ladies Singles Champion - Ann Jones - United Kingdom

The 1969 Wimbledon Championships took place on the outdoor grass courts at the All England Lawn Tennis and Croquet Club in Wimbledon, London, and ran from the 23rd June until the 5th July. It was the 83rd staging of the Wimbledon Championships and the third Grand Slam tennis event of 1969. *Fun Fact: During a first round match 41-year-old Pancho Gonzalez beat Charlie Pasarell by a score of 22-24, 1-6, 16-14, 6-3 and 11-9. At 112 games and 5 hours 20 minutes it was by far the longest match of the time and led to the introduction of the tiebreak in tennis.*

Men's Singles Final:

Country	Player	Set 1	Set 2	Set 3	Set 4
Australia	Rod Laver	6	5	6	6
Australia	John Newcombe	4	7	4	4

Women's Singles Final:

Country	Player	Set 1	Set 2	Set 3
United Kingdom	Ann Jones	3	6	6
United States	Billie Jean King	6	3	2

Men's Doubles Final:

Country	Players	Set 1	Set 2	Set 3
Australia	John Newcombe / Tony Roche	7	11	6
Netherlands / United States	Tom Okker / Marty Riessen,	5	9	3

Women's Doubles Final:

Country	Players	Set 1	Set 2
Australia	Margaret Court / Judy Tegart	9	6
United States	Patti Hogan / Peggy Michel	7	2

Mixed Doubles Final:

Country	Players	Set 1	Set 2
Australia / United Kingdom	Fred Stolle / Ann Jones	6	6
Australia	Tony Roche / Judy Tegart	2	3

County Championship Cricket Winners

GLAMORGAN

1969 saw the 70th officially organised running of the County Championship. Glamorgan won the Championship title in a season which saw games played reduced from 28 to 24.

Pos.	Team	Pld.	W	L	D	Pts.
1	**Glamorgan**	**24**	**11**	**0**	**13**	**250**
2	Gloucestershire	24	10	6	8	219
3	Surrey	24	7	1	16	210
4	Warwickshire	24	7	3	14	205
5	Hampshire	24	6	7	11	203

N.B. The Sunday League (now the National League) began in 1969. All matches were played on Sundays with each of the 17 first-class counties playing each other once.

Test Series Cricket

Pakistan vs England
Series drawn 0-0

Test	Dates	Ground	Result
1st Test	21st Feb - 24th Feb	Lahore Stadium, Lahore	Match drawn
2nd Test	28th Feb - 3rd Mar	Dacca Stadium, Dacca	Match drawn
3rd Test	6th Mar - 8th Mar	National Stadium, Karachi	Match drawn

England vs West Indies
England win 2-0

Test	Dates	Ground	Result
1st Test	12th Jun - 17th Jun	Old Trafford, Manchester	England won by 10 wickets
2nd Test	26th Jun - 1st Jul	Lord's, London	Match drawn
3rd Test	10th Jul - 15th Jul	Headingley, Leeds	England won by 30 runs

England vs New Zealand
England win 2-0

Test	Dates	Ground	Result
1st Test	24th Jul - 28th Jul	Lord's, London	England won by 230 runs
2nd Test	7th Aug - 12th Aug	Trent Bridge, Nottingham	Match drawn
3rd Test	21st Aug - 26th Aug	The Oval, London	England won by 8 wickets

THE COST OF LIVING

COMPARISON CHART

	1969 Price	1969 (+ Inflation)	2018 Price	% Change
3 Bedroom House	£5,700	£94,153	£227,874	+142%
Weekly Income	£12.8s.2d	£204.96	£535	+161%
Pint Of Beer	1s.3d	£1.03	£3.60	+249.5%
Cheese (lb)	5s.4d	£4.40	£3.38	-23.2%
Bacon (lb)	7s.5d	£6.13	£3.34	-45.5%
The Beano	4d	28p	£2.50	+792.9%

SHOPPING

Golden Meadow Butter (1lb)	2s.8d
Kangaroo Butter (1lb)	3s
Kraft Family Margarine (1lb)	1s.7d
Australian Cheddar Cheese (1lb)	2s.6d
Branston Pickle (11oz jar)	1s.8d
White Potatoes (5lb bag)	1s.10d
Geest Bananas (per lb)	1s
Jaffa Oranges (each)	8d
New Zealand Leg Of Lamb (per lb)	4s.6d
Quality Brand Chicken (per lb)	2s.6d
Plumrose Chopped Ham & Pork (12oz)	4s
Fray Bentos Corned Beef (7oz)	2s.9d
John West Pilchards (7½oz)	1s.1d
Heinz Baked Beans (16oz tin)	1s
Farrow's Marrowfat Peas (10½oz)	7d
Nescafe Coffee (2oz)	2s.6d
PG Tips (½lb)	1s.5d
Sainbury's Red Label Tea (4oz)	1s.3d
Nestle's Ideal Evaporated Milk (14½oz)	1s.2d
Sugrosa Sweetener (100)	2s.9d
Robinsons Orange / Lemon Drink (bottle)	2s.2d
Schweppes Lemonade (8½fl.oz bottle)	11d
Kellogg's Corn Flakes (12oz)	1s.6d
Quaker Oats (pkt.)	1s.8d
Robertson's Mince Meat (14½oz jar)	1s.8d
Golden Shred Marmalade (1lb)	1s.7d
Jacob's Cream Crackers	10d
Ritz Crackers	1s.4d
Ryvita (packet)	1s
Sainbury's Sliced Peaches (15oz)	1s.5d
Ambrosia Creamed Rice (15½oz tin)	1s
Bird's Trifle	1s.11d
Bird's Custard	1s.5d
Chivers Jelly	9d
After Eight Chocolates	4s.4d
Cadbury's Fingers (8oz pkt.)	2s.8d
McVite's Jaffa Cakes	1s.7d
Cedar Wood Pre-Electric Shave	7s.6d
Brylcreem (medium size)	3s.6d
Gon Chilblain Tablets (pocket size)	3s
Optrex	3s.10d
Andrex 2 Roll Economy Pack	1s.5½d
Baco Foil	2s
Parozone Bleach (32oz)	1s.2d
Pedigree Chum (large size)	1s.6d
Winalot Meal Dog Food (large)	1s.11d
Paws Cat Food (small)	10d
Daily Tibs - Vitamin/Mineral Tablets For Cats (30)	2s.6d

CLOTHES

Women's Clothing

Montrose Dress 'n Trouser Suit	£3.9s.6d
Valuwear White Collar Dress	£1.5s
Ambrose Wilson Pop Over	£2.19s.11d
R.J. Wiltshire Crimplene Lined Skirt	£2.7s.6d
Lilian Fenton Quality Stretch Nylon Girdle	19s.6d
Pretty Polly Leprechaun Pantihose	9s
Fine Fare 'One Size' Stockings	2s.6d
Big M Slippers	from 4s.11d

Men's Clothing

Alexandre Overcoat	£9.10s
Burton's Suit	from £10.19s.6d
Hardy Amies Tailored Jacket	£8.5s
Yorkers Terylene Trousers	from £3.3s

TOYS

B.S.A. Wayfarer Boys Bicycle	£17.17s
Halfords Mayflower Girls Bicycle	£14.15s
901 Drag Kart	£12.19s.6d
Woolworth's Pedal Jeep	£4.19s.6d
Kiddie Trike	£3.15s.6d
Woolworth's Dolls Pram	£4.19s.6d
Toddler Baby Walker With Plastic Blocks	£3.2s.6d
Jacko The Monkey	£2.9s.11d
Winfield 'Race Away' Racing Set	£2.2s.6d
Hot Wheels	5s.11d
Scrabble	£1.10s.6d
Spearoscope	19s.11d
Spear's Coppit Chase Game	12s

JOE 90 NEW

DINKY TOYS

5½" (139 mm.)

102 Joe's Car

* AUTOMATIC OPENING WINGS AND EXTENDING TAIL FINS
* FLASHING ENGINE EXHAUST
* INDEPENDENT SUPER SUSPENSION

100 Lady Penelope's FAB 1

5½" (143 mm.)

5½" (147 mm.)

Straight from **THUNDERBIRDS**

101 Thunderbird II

Joe 90 Car - 25s.11d / Lady Penelope's FAB 1 - 16s.11d / Thunderbird 2 - 14s.11d

ELECTRICAL ITEMS

Pye CT 70 25in Colour TV	£345.16s.2d
Bush CTV 174 D 22in Colour TV	£304.15s.2d
Granada Weekly TV Rental	from 8s.4d
Bush Record Player	29½gns
Bush Radio	9½gns
Philips Twin-Turbo Fan Heater	£6.19s.6d
Philips Food Mixer	£8.8s
Morphy Richards Toaster	£6.15s
Termozeta Hair Dryer	£2.19s.6d
Carmen Heated Hair Rollers	15gns
Morphy Richards 1kw De Luxe Heater	£3.4s.6d
Singer 359 Sewing Machine	£35.13s.6d
Hoover Steam Iron	£3.19s.6d
Black & Decker 14in Wood Turning Lathe	£3.15s
Skil Power Drill	£7.10s
Black & Decker Power Hedge Trimmer	£7.19s.6d

OTHER PRICES

Lotus Elan +2S Car	£2,375
Austin Maxi Car	£978.16s.11d
Renault 6 Car	£725
Super-Rail/Overland Holiday To Tossa De Mar, Spain	£32.0s.6d
Riviera Jet Flight To Majorca	from 28gns
Silver Mist Imperial Shed 7ft x 5ft	£20.10s
Medi Victor Frame Tent 14ft x 8ft x 7ft	£28.10s
Qualcast Superlite Panther Lawn Mower	£8.9s.9d
Super Rotary Clothes Airer	£3.15s
Mayfair Quilted Studio Couch	£18.18s
MFI New Home Desk	£4.15s
Slumberland Purple Seal 4ft 6in Divan	£36.7s.6d
50-Piece Stainless Steel Swedish Pattern Cutlery Set	£2.14s.6d
Mayoral Super 8 Cine Camera	£19.19s
Kodak Instamatic 33 Camera	£3.19s.6d
Lieberman & Gortz 7x35 Binoculars	£12.19s
Prismatic Compass	£2.5s
H. Samuel Everite Gold Plated Watch	£10.10s
Martell Cognac (large bottle)	£3.15s.9d
International Spanish Wines	10s.6d
Player's No.10 Cigarettes (20)	3s.6d
Guards Big Size Cigarettes (20)	4s.10d
Embassy Gold Cigarettes (20)	3s.10d
Golden Virginia Rolling Tobacco (½oz)	3s.6d
Knowledge Children's Magazine	2s.6d
Reveille Magazine	6d

BEST BUY DIPLOMAT

Today it makes more good sense than ever to choose Diplomat. Firmly filled with the same superb tobaccos used in more expensive cigarettes. Packed in a smart crush-proof box. Only

3/8*
for 20

WILLS ⚜

pacemakers in tobacco

Recommended price

WD55

MONEY CONVERSION TABLE

Old Money		Equivalent
Farthing	¼d	0.1p
Half Penny	½d	0.21p
Penny	1d	0.42p
Threepence	3d	1.25p
Sixpence	6d	2.5p
Shilling	1s	5p
Florin	2s	10p
Half Crown	2s.6d	12.5p
Crown	5s	25p
Ten Shillings	10s	50p
Pound	20s	£1
Guinea	21s	£1.05

Our best advertisement yet.

So far, we haven't succeeded in producing a better advertisement for the Cortina 1600E, than the 1600E itself.

E, by the way, stands for Executive. But, as 'Motor' Magazine pointed out, it can also stand for Enthusiast or Extrovert.

And the 1600E has enough performance and polish to satisfy the most extroverted executive.

To get this result, we started with the Cortina. Which was a very good start indeed.

Because the Cortina is probably the most perfectly designed family car ever made. And it has won more than its fair share of races and rallies.

Out of those races and rallies came a lot of exciting developments. All of which went into the development of the 1600E.

There's the 1600cc GT engine that gives you 92bhp at 5400rpm and takes you from 0-60mph in 11.8 seconds.

There's the special close-ratio gearbox (which many motoring magazines consider to be one of the best in the world) with its stubby, close-to-hand, gearlever.

There's the lowered, firmer, suspension and the fat 5½″ wheels with radial-ply tyres to give you fantastic handling and roadholding.

There are the paired driving lamps and twin automatic reversing lamps. The aluminium alloy steering wheel with leather covered rim. The contoured bucket seats to give you a firm, relaxed, driving position.

(In fact, there are bucket seats all round to keep your passengers just as comfortable as you. And a 21 cu. ft. boot because we reckon a car that can carry 5 people should be able to carry more than 2 people's luggage.)

Having got all the practical parts right, we then felt free to indulge in a few extravagant touches.

Like putting in a polished walnut facia and door cappings. Fully reclining front seats. An electric clock in the centre console. Luxurious cut-pile carpet. And a cigar lighter.

Altogether it's quite a car. It would be hard for us to find a better advertisement.

And just as hard for you to find a better car.

Ford leads the way.

CORTINA 1600E

CARTOONS

"Hold it! I had it upside down—they want a well!"

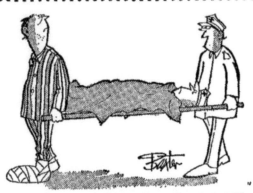

"Marvellous how lightning 'flu strikes, isn't it?"

"I just bought it, officer— in Carnaby Street!"

"No man's standing on a pedestal while we're around!"

Printed in Great
Britain
by Amazon